MW01137485

"Not Tonight, Honey"

Handling Your Wife's Sexual
Rejection

Rob Green

New
Growth
Press

www.newgrowthpress.com

New Growth Press, Greensboro, NC 27404
www.newgrowthpress.com

Cover Design: Tandem Creative, Tom Temple, tandemcreative.net
Typesetting: Lisa Parnell, lparnell.com

ISBN 13: 978-1-936768-64-6
ISBN-13: 978-1-938267-42-0 (eBook)

        Library of Congress Cataloging-in-Publication Data
Green, Rob (Robert Eric)
  Not tonight, honey : handling your wife's sexual rejection / Rob
Green.
      p. cm.
  Includes bibliographical references and index.
  ISBN 13: 978-1-936768-64-6 (alk. paper)
  1. Sex—Religious aspects—Christianity. 2. Sex in marriage—
Religious aspects—Christianity. 3. Wives—Sexual behavior.
I. Title.
  BT708.G685   2012
  248.8'425—dc23
                                                        2012024297
Printed in Canada

21 20 19 18 17 16 15 14   3 4 5 6 7

N ot tonight, honey"[1] must be three of the most annoying words a husband can ever hear.

You can probably think back to several times you heard those words and the events preceding them. You kissed your wife goodbye before you left for work. On occasional breaks you sent her a quick e-mail or text telling her that you loved her. You imagined the kids going to bed on time so that you and your wife could have some enjoyable time together, including sex. What happened? Everything was going according to plan until the "enjoyable time together" part. She wanted to go to bed! You couldn't believe it. Bed! Seriously? Hello, Mr. Wonderful is here and the kids are asleep. Even now, you can feel your blood pressure rising and your irritation building.

Or what about the time she texted you to say that she couldn't wait for you to come home. You almost left the office right then. You were ready to cancel your meetings, and you could have been half undressed before you pulled in the driveway. But you restrained yourself. Instead, you flirted a little throughout the day as you looked forward to the evening ahead. Unfortunately, by the time dinner was finished, homework was completed, baths were given, and bedtime stories were read, she was exhausted. Her flirting was gone, and she was simply too tired. You thought to yourself that she had energy for dinner, for the kids, and for everything she did through the day—except you! It was irritating, really irritating!

I'm not sure I have met a married man who hasn't experienced moments like these. I suspect you are reading this book because you know exactly what I'm talking about. So what should you do? How should you respond when your wife says "not tonight"?

I think you know that God is not pleased when you respond with outbursts of sinful anger, or manipulative ploys to get your wife to change her mind, or even self-pity that changes "not tonight" to "hardly ever" in your private thoughts. We all know there is a better way—a biblical way. Remember that when the Lord saved you, he wanted you to find your identity in Jesus, to live in ways pleasing to him, and to enjoy him beginning right now.

The question is really how you can do all that when you are faced with sexual disappointment. Let me say from the beginning that it is possible to respond in a way that honors God and that allows your marriage to be a picture of Christ's love for his church. Here are four biblical principles that can greatly help you respond to those irritating "not tonight" moments with the grace of Jesus.

Respond to your rejection the way Jesus responded to his

Christ's earthly sufferings can teach you a lot about how to respond to your disappointment. Certainly his suffering and rejection far exceed what you face when your wife is not interested in sex, so I'm not making a one-to-one comparison. But it helps to know that Jesus really understands rejection *and* that his death on the cross gives you what you need to deal with it as he did.

Let's consider some of the things Jesus suffered. According to Matthew, people mocked him as he hung on the cross: "If you are the Son of God, come down from the cross"; "He saved others; he cannot save himself" (27:40–42). Despite the mockery and rejection, Jesus' response was to offer his life.

Do you remember what happened earlier, in the garden of Gethsemane? The disciples fell asleep even after Jesus asked them to watch and pray with him (Matthew 26:36–46). Later, Peter denied Jesus three times, and at least the last denial was within Jesus' hearing (Matthew 26:69–75; Luke 22:61).

In addition to the suffering of his Passion Week, the Gospels record hostile reactions toward Jesus by the crowds throughout his ministry. Despite it all Jesus responded with compassion and grace. Apart from the false teachers themselves, Jesus responded to people's rejection with compassion and kindness. He saw the multitudes as sheep without a shepherd. He responded with compassion to the lame, the sick, and the hurting.

At the cross Jesus responded with compassion toward those who were watching and sneering, and to all of us as well. Romans 5:8 uses the phrase "while we were yet sinners" to remind us that Jesus died for people who were in rebellion against him. Jesus died for *you* while you were an enemy, while you were a rebel, and while you sinned against him. In other words, Jesus died so that you would be rescued from the power and penalty of sin. You were rescued so that you would have an identity firmly rooted in his finished work. With that new identity as a child of God comes a new heart, empowered by the Holy Spirit to love and serve as Jesus did.

The implications for your life seem clear, don't they? In those moments when your wife is not interested in your sexual advances (for whatever reason), you are to respond with grace, compassion, and kindness. Obviously, your challenge is not nearly as significant as the ones borne by your Savior, but how you respond is important to God. God can use your response to disappointment, rejection and suffering—at whatever level—to help you understand his love and change you to be more like him, and to reflect those changes in the way you love your wife. This puts the challenge of "not tonight, honey" in a whole new perspective.

I am not simply suggesting that you "man up" and

quit whining. Instead, I am encouraging you to find the strength to live for Christ based on your position in Christ and the ministry of the Spirit living in you. Just as Christ rescued you from the power of sin, he can rescue you from ungodly responses to your spouse in the midst of disappointment.

Honestly, becoming like Jesus does not simply happen by listening to a sermon, attending a small group, or being taught truth. Becoming like Jesus also happens when you respond in a Christ-like way, through the power of the Spirit, to situations and circumstances you do not like. Christian growth occurs in the moment-by-moment decisions of your everyday life. Will grace, compassion, and kindness win because you are relying on the work of God in your life? Or will selfishness, irritation, and anger win because you are relying on your own strength?

Men, I think responding to your wife as Jesus would eliminates

- Sighing as you roll over to go to sleep.
- Giving her the "cold shoulder" once you realize that sex is not in the plans.
- Complaining and grumbling, even in your thoughts.
- Waking up the next morning in a foul mood and blaming her for that attitude.

Responses filled with grace, compassion, and kindness might involve

- Giving your wife affection even though you know it will not end in sex.
- Telling her that you love her, giving her a goodnight kiss, and then calmly rolling over.
- Rejoicing that you had the opportunity to love your wife when it was challenging.

Men, we are commanded to love our wives as Christ loves the church (Ephesians 5:25). Obedience to that command involves responding with grace, compassion, and kindness when we are disappointed. Jesus knew how to respond to rejection, and we need to learn to do the same. In addition to responding as Jesus would, let me also encourage you to think about "not tonight, honey" as an opportunity.

Don't think about what you lost, but about the opportunity you've gained

I am always amazed by Philippians 1:12–14. We know from history that Paul was imprisoned under house arrest for three to four years when he wrote this letter. After that much time you would think Paul would be frustrated, irritated, and discouraged. But Paul was able to see his imprisonment as an opportunity. He said his imprisonment resulted in the further progress of the gospel. Despite his difficult circumstances, Paul saw opportunity where others saw hardship. He was able to choose "what is excellent" (Philippians 1:9–11).

Paul's sufferings exceed our own. Marriage has, by design, some opportunities for disappointment. Any time two sinners, even those saved by grace, live together in marriage, there will be times of discord. By God's grace you will be able to look for the opportunity, as Paul did, when faced with one of the built-in challenges of marriage—"not tonight."

On one side of the equation we know that "not tonight" will result in a loss of pleasure, just as Paul lost his freedom while imprisoned. God, in his sovereignty, designed sex to be physically, emotionally, and spiritually enjoyable. But the greater pleasure always comes from living a life worthy of the gospel, which is what Paul was able to do as he wrote Philippians. The greatest joy comes as we choose to desire the things God desires. It comes as we choose the path of a gospel-centered life of thankfulness, faith, and submission to Christ rather than the path of rebellion, which results in dishonor to Christ. This means that doing what is right ultimately results in the greater pleasure. Let's see how this works in a real-life situation.

Brian desires sex with his wife Brooke. She, at least tonight, is not particularly interested. Brian, however, convinces himself that she wants sex too—she just hasn't figured it out yet. So Brian shaves, takes a shower, uses the cologne she likes best, brushes his teeth, and dons clothing she normally finds attractive. By the time he is done, he is absolutely convinced that her "not tonight" will be replaced by a speedy retreat to the bedroom. But this time his plan does not work. Brooke is still not interested, and she is a little irritated that he went to all that trouble. Brian marches off, clearly frustrated. When they get into the bedroom, however, Brooke has a slight change of heart. She knows that Brian made an effort and he will probably be upset about it tomorrow, so she gives in. Brian won—or did he? Yes, he received the physical pleasure that comes with sex. But what did that cost? You see, Brian thought that "what is excellent" (extrapolating from Philippians) was sex. What he missed was that the truly excellent thing was an opportunity to really love and care for Brooke.

In this scenario both Brian and Brooke lost. They lost because at the heart of their sexual relations was manipulation. Their union was not strengthened; it was compromised. Their sex life did not get stronger because it was being built on love, trust, and security; instead, it was a tool for their own pleasure. Brian got sex. Brooke does not have to deal with a whiny Brian in the morning. Their relationship took a step in the wrong direction. They completely missed "what is excellent."

If we change this scenario and allow Brian to choose the excellent thing, we can also see the value of the results. For example, if Brian had chosen to clean up the house, encourage Brooke to rest, and pray with her, notice how the results would have been different.

- Brian would have lost the pleasure of sex, but he would have gained the joy that comes from living for Jesus. With this choice Brian exchanged the lesser joy for the greater joy.
- Brian did not manipulate Brooke, but instead loved and cared for her in the midst of her fatigue. Brian became a hero to his wife, rather than a manipulator.
- Brian may not realize it, but by showing himself to be kind and compassionate he made it easier for Brooke to respond to future sexual advances. Many women pray for their husbands to be tender, loving, understanding, and kind.
- Brian was learning one of the key disciplines of a good sexual relationship—the importance of being pleasing to the other person.

Guys, I am probably going to step on a few toes with this one, but don't worry because I had to step on my own first. Are you affectionate with your wife when sex will not be part of the plan? Better yet, what happens when you are really affectionate with your wife and she still wants to sleep? When you are affectionate with your wife your sexual desires ramp up, but sometimes hers do not. Can you, in that moment, be affectionate and loving and still choose to roll over nicely and sleep? We men sometimes fail to realize that we communicate a very positive message to our wives when we are affectionate without sex. We show them that we love them, not just their bodies. Although these are times when you will not get what you desire, these are also times to remember that you gained more in your relationship than you lost.

Men, the words "not tonight" are a huge opportunity for you to choose the excellent thing and to see the progress of your relationship, much like Paul chose the excellent thing and saw the progress of the gospel. Yes, you will lose the physical pleasure that comes from sex (keep in mind that Paul had no freedom for a much longer time), but you will gain so much more. You will not only experience the joy of the Lord, but you will strengthen your marriage. Over time, a strengthened marriage often results in an improved sex life with your spouse.

Establish safety and security in your relationship

In 1 Corinthians 7:3–5, we are told that sex involves mutual authority. The husband's body is not his own, nor is the wife's body her own. Each one is encouraged to use their bodies to bless their spouse, to agree to serve the other in this way. Notice that Paul teaches this is a "giving" by each person, not a forcing of sexual relations by the other. In addition to the basic idea of mutual consent, there is another important implication of 1 Corinthians 7:3–5—namely, that safety and security should be established in your relationship. These two elements are crucial for developing a godly sexual relationship.

Think for a moment about why people in our culture wear clothes. I think part of the answer is that nakedness makes you vulnerable. If you accidentally walk into the opposite sex's locker room, you will watch everyone scurry for towels as you try to get out as fast as possible. If you watch a teen lose his shorts, the first thing he does is reach for them. Why? There is no safety or security in those moments. You just hope your picture does not end up on YouTube!

This idea has implications for marriage. For a husband and wife to enjoy sexual intimacy there must be safety and security in the relationship. The wife cannot wonder whether he thinks she is attractive. She cannot think, *I wonder if he thinks I'm fat?* or *I wonder if he has noticed that I have gained ten pounds this year?* Her thoughts cannot be, *I wonder what kind of criticism I will get if I do not do my part right?* or *I wonder if he only stays with me for sex?* And she cannot focus on, *I wonder what we will argue about tonight?* Safety and security are necessary in a close relationship. Let me highlight a few ways in which these qualities can be eroded.

1. If you criticize as much or more than you compliment, you do not have safety and security in the relationship. Some men are quite frankly jerks. They whine, complain, try to "fix" stuff about their wives, and then wonder why their wives are not interested in sex. Seriously? Who wants to have sex with your worst critic? So I want to encourage you to evaluate your relationship. Is it characterized by criticism? Some men complain about the cooking and the cleaning and everything in between. Is your demeanor such that even thankfulness seems cheap or insincere? Some men compliment but, when they do, it almost seems fake.

I encourage you to ask your wife to be honest about your relationship. Does she view you as one who encourages her, supports her, loves her, and cares about her wants and needs, or does she view you as selfish? Does she think of herself as your wife, partner, lover, and life companion? Or are you so critical that she thinks you treat her like a child, or as a mere servant or secretary?

My point is simple: there is no safety or security in a relationship based on criticism.

2. If you do not thank her for sex but simply expect it, you do not have safety and security in the relationship. This point is related to the first one, but it applies directly to your sexual relationship. Some men think about sex in terms of "rights and duty." It is their "right" to get sex and their wives' "duty" to perform it. Though there is a grain of biblical truth in that, this attitude twists what Scripture says and makes sex something far less than God designed it to be. Sex is supposed to be about mutual love and mutual pleasure. If that is true, why can't we be thankful to our wives? Why can't we be appreciative?

My guess, men, is that you either have or have had a boss who annoyed you. What you did was never good enough. He viewed you through the grid of duty, and you rarely, if ever, lived up to his expectations. Why didn't he thank you for your efforts? Simple— he wasn't thankful. His heart was filled with duty and expectation. Do you remember how much safety and security you had in that relationship? Now think about your wife. If you aren't thanking her for your times of intimacy, it is because your heart is not very thankful. It is because you see her through the grid of duty, and maybe she is not living up to her duty from your point of view. How much safety and security does she have in your relationship? None, zero, zilch. You need a heart transplant. You need the duty, rights, and expectations heart replaced with a heart of thankfulness.

Without a heart of thankfulness, you will not have safety and security.

3. If she can honestly never say "no" without you having an adult temper tantrum, you do not have safety and security in the relationship. Your wife needs to be able to say no sometimes without you having adult fits. (You need to be able to say no too, though some of us might wonder why you would!) I have heard about these adult temper tantrums. The husband begins by rolling over and breathing deeply with the occasional sigh. When asked if anything is wrong, he says "Oh, nothing." Some husbands angrily grab the covers and roll over, pouting like a two-year-old. Some who have learned that sex will not happen that evening go to bed two hours early, justifying it with some lame excuse about being tired—after all, they worked all day. Do you see how this is counter to 1 Corinthians 7:3–4? Do you see how this is counter to your overall walk with Jesus? Do you see that the implications of the gospel would lead you to an entirely different response? Don't you see what this is doing to your wife and your relationship?

Someone who really understands what Jesus has done for him is overwhelmed with gratitude for his salvation. This makes it much easier to accept, with genuine joy, the reality that sex will not always occur when he (or she) wants it. The person can be joyful because he knows that God is using this particular disappointment to produce in him the kind of character that honors Christ (Romans 5:3–5; James 1:2–4).

If your wife cannot honestly say no, you do not have safety and security.

4. If you are manipulating your wife for sex, you do not have safety and security in the relationship. Another tactic some Christian men use to get sex is manipulation. What makes this so twisted is that some of the manipulative comments contain elements of biblical truth. For example, what if you told your wife that it is much easier for you to avoid temptation when she has sex with you? There is *some* biblical truth to that (1 Corinthians 7:5). But some men use that statement to lay heavy guilt-trip burdens on their wives. They take the Word of God and twist it for their own manipulative purposes. Guys, this is sin on your part. If you honestly believe that your ability to resist temptation is based on your wife's willingness to have sex, then this minibook is not enough for you. Please take it with you to your pastor and get more help.

Another way that some men manipulate their wives is more subtle. If their wives refuse their requests for sex, some men become very hesitant to initiate sex again. Some go to the extreme of forcing their wives to do all the initiating. This results in a frustrating situation that helps neither person honor Christ. When men hear their wives say "not tonight," this temporary rejection should not cause them to lose their masculinity and give up pursuing their wives. That is not God's plan for marriage. Men, if you are prone to this line of thinking, it is time to find your identity and confidence in Jesus rather than in your wife's sexual responses or lack of them. Tonight might not work out as you have planned, but if your identity and focus are on Christ, you will respond in the power of the Spirit rather than in the weakness of the flesh.

To this point I have challenged you 1) To respond to rejection and disappointment with love, grace, and compassion, responding in the power of the Spirit just as Jesus did in the midst of his rejection; 2) To view "not tonight" as an opportunity rather than a disappointment through the power of Christ, just as Paul did in far more difficult circumstances; and 3) To establish safety and security in your relationship. That brings me to the final point.

As appropriate, lovingly confront

I can almost hear some of you being incredibly frustrated with me. "Rob, you don't know my wife. If I did not push her for sex, we would never have it!" or "Rob, she uses those words to manipulate the fire out of me." I realize that some men have married women who rarely, if ever, initiate. I realize that some men have wives who have somehow been convinced that sex is bad, dirty, or to be avoided at all costs. Let me give you three responses to these objections.

1. That is not true for many men, including many of you reading this minibook. The reality is that you have not been a good spiritual leader. You have not loved your wife adequately, and your sex life is symptomatic of a larger marriage problem. You might be surprised at how a little biblical love and Christ-like attitude on your part translate into more frequency in the bedroom on her part. This does not mean that two weeks of being nice to your wife fixes your marriage, for that is manipulation, but you becoming more like Jesus will help your wife respond with more affection.

2. Matthew 7:3–5 says that we are to remove the log in our own eye before we attempt to remove the speck in someone else's. The point Jesus made is that we always need to look first at our own life before we make accusations about the lives of others. You need to see yourself as having the log. Look for ways that

the gospel of Christ can drive your response. That is the primary reason that the first three principles—1) responding to rejection, 2) thinking about what you gained, and 3) establishing safety and security—are about you.

3. Remember that whenever there is a problem between two people, each person can decide to be part of the solution or part of the problem. We hope you choose to be part of the solution.

Having said all this, it is possible that some of you have wives who regularly use various excuses to avoid sex. If you both were honest, you would have to conclude that she is living in 1 Corinthians 7:5—she is depriving you. This situation is different from the situation I have addressed. Not only do you have the responsibility to live in God's grace and to extend that grace to your wife, but now you must also lovingly confront her about her sin as well. You must confront her because you want her to live a life pleasing to Jesus, you want her to give a good account at the judgment seat of Christ, and you want your relationship to be all that God intended.

After you have prayerfully thought this through, after you have taken the earlier steps, and after you have been quick to ask forgiveness for any failings you have had, then you may begin to discuss the difficulty. Whenever confronting your wife about sex, there are several important things to remember.

1. Ask questions rather than make accusations. Saying, "It seems to me that you do not have much interest in sex. Can you please help me understand why?" is different from "You know, I read this little book that gave me lots of ideas on how to respond when you don't want sex. I have been doing those things. What is your deal?"

2. Make the confrontation about Scripture, not just what you want. Many couples have to figure out details about sex as they go along in their marriage. This discussion is not about a preference; it is about whether there is a sin issue between your spouse and God. Use Scripture to encourage your wife to live for Jesus, and explain that sex is part of her living wholeheartedly for Christ. It may be that your sexual difficulties reveal a larger heart issue for your wife. For example, she may believe that sex is dirty and unbecoming for a Christian wife. She may have been sexually victimized in the past and never worked it through. She may have regrets in this area

of her life. Or she simply may not understand what it means to be in union with Christ, to be loved by Jesus more than anyone could possibly love her, or what it looks like to live in the power of the Spirit in the sexual area of life. Your sexual problems could allow you to love her as Christ loves the church in the most profound way of all—helping her grow to be more like her Savior.

3. Look for steps of growth but also exercise patience. The Lord is very patient with all of us. Therefore, you must exercise patience with your wife. Remember that while you exercise patience, God is giving you grace. Your sex life may not be what you hoped it would be, but by God's grace you are choosing to live worthy of the gospel, and that is the greatest joy.

The goal of confrontation is not simply to point out sin; it is to live in a way that is pleasing to Jesus and to be reconciled through confession and forgiveness. Please do not use this time to merely rebuke your wife. Help her see the great value and joy of truly living for Jesus in this area, and help her deal with any obstacles she faces.

Conclusions

Men, hearing the words "not tonight" is annoying and frustrating, but it can be one of the greatest opportunities to serve your wife, to live worthy of the gospel, and to love her like Christ loves the church. Before we blame our wives, let's make sure that we are living worthy of the gospel and in the power of the Spirit. This looks like responding first with grace, compassion, and patience. After all, there may be many reasons why "tomorrow" might work a lot better. Rather than getting angry or bitter, it is important to respond to your rejection the way Christ responded to his—through the power of the Spirit.

In addition, let's remember that responding with grace means that you give and serve rather than take and demand. Responding in a godly way communicates to your wife that you are interested in her wants, desires, and needs. Yes, you lose sex for the evening, but you gain much more in your relationship with her. You show her that you are interested in being, with God's help, an Ephesians 5 Christian husband. You desire to walk in love (5:2) and to love her as Christ loves the church (5:25).

Then, please seek to build safety and security in your relationship with your wife. The safer and more secure she is in your relationship, the more fulfilling your sexual intimacy will be. Seeking safety and security through an open and honest relationship, with the ability to say no on occasion, is much more Christ-like than the manipulation, anger, complaints, and ungratefulness that characterize so many men.

After you have put all these steps into practice and sought to honor the Lord, then you may lovingly confront your wife if "not tonight" is sin on her part. After all, the Lord might use you to help her learn about her identity in Christ, about how Christ loves her, and about what it means to live worthy of the gospel. Then you would be loving her as Jesus loves his bride, the church, tonight and every night.

Endnotes

1. Maybe it goes without saying, but there are clearly limits to this minibook. I assume that you and your wife are capable of sexual intercourse. I assume that neither of you has a medical condition or injury that prevents you from engaging in sex. I also assume that sexual intercourse is physically pleasurable to you both. If sexual intercourse is extremely painful for your wife, other issues need to be addressed that are beyond the scope of this work. Therefore, if you are incapable of sex or sex is physically painful, please see your doctor. It might also be helpful to talk with your pastor or nearest biblical counselor to receive specific help for some of your challenges.